Reduce, Reuse, Recycle, Replace!

By George Ivanoff

AF583670

Pearson Australia
(a division of Pearson Australia Group Pty Ltd)
707 Collins Street, Melbourne, Victoria 3008
PO Box 23360, Melbourne, Victoria 8012
www.pearson.com.au

First published 2014 by Pearson Australia
2020 2019 2018 2017
10 9 8 7 6 5 4 3 2 1

Publisher: Dian Faulisi
Project Manager: Michelle Thomas
Editor: Petra Poupa
Cover & Series Designers: Jenny Grigg and Anne Donald
Designer: Norma van Rees
Copyright & Pictures Editor: Katy Murenu
Mac Operator: Rob Curulli
Illustrator: Fiona Lee
Printed in Australia by the SOS Print + Media Group

ISBN 978 1 4860 0845 2
Pearson Australia Group Pty Ltd ABN 40 004 245 943

Acknowledgements
We would like to thank the following for permission to reproduce copyright material.
The following abbreviations are used in this list: t = top, b = bottom, l = left, r = right, c = centre.

Fotolia: pp. 12bl, 13br, back cover.
Getty Images: Mike Clarke, p. 7bl; Brooke Slezak, p. 6bl; Image Source, p. Cover; Science Photo Library, p. 7br, 9.
Shutterstock: pp. 1, 3, 4(all), 5, 6tr, 6br, 7tr, 8, 10, 11, 12tr, 12br, 13tr, 14(all), 15, 16(all), 17(all), 18tr, 19, 20, 22.

Every effort has been made to trace and acknowledge copyright. However, should any infringement have occurred, the publishers tender their apologies and invite copyright owners to contact them.

Disclaimer
Some of the images used in *Reduce, Reuse, Recycle, Replace!* might have associations with deceased Indigenous Australians. Please be aware that these images might cause sadness or distress in Aboriginal or Torres Strait Islander communities.

Contents

What a waste!

Every day people throw out bin loads of rubbish. Much of it is disposed of thoughtlessly, even though it could still be used, reused or recycled. Not all waste is useless.

Vegetable scraps can be **composted**. Paper, metal and plastic can be recycled. Some items can even be reused in new ways. There is so much that can be done to reduce the amount of waste that we throw out.

Here are four important words to remember:

REDUCE: use fewer products to create less waste
REUSE: reuse products rather than throwing them out
RECYCLE: recycle products so that they can be made into something new
REPLACE: replace **non-renewable** resources with **renewable** ones

We can make better choices! Next time you go to throw something into a bin, stop and think first.

LET'S FIND OUT

- **What is waste?**
- **What happens to waste in nature?**
- **What happens to the rubbish you throw out?**
- **Why is recycling important?**
- **What can you do to reduce waste?**

Plastics can be recycled and reused in interesting ways.

Rubbish

When you throw something into a rubbish bin, what happens to it?

Rubbish is collected in large trucks and taken to a rubbish tip where it is compacted – squashed – so that it takes up less space. The compacted rubbish is then buried. This buried rubbish is called landfill.

A rubbish tip is usually a gigantic hole in the ground. Each day, rubbish is dumped into it and covered with a layer of soil.

Did you know?
According to the Australian Bureau of Statistics, in 2009–2010 Australians sent 21.6 million tonnes of rubbish to landfill.

Household rubbish goes into the bin.

The rubbish is put outside for collection.

Landfill gets rid of rubbish, but there are problems with the system.

It is expensive. Each year, millions of dollars are spent on collecting, transporting and burying rubbish.

Landfill **pollutes** the air and the surrounding soil and water. Rubbish tips also smell pretty bad.

Sadly, many of the things that people throw out should not be put into landfill. Used batteries, for example, leak poison into the ground. Any **organic** matter that is put into landfill is wasted and many items could be reused instead of being thrown out.

It is also difficult to find new landfill sites. Most people don't want a rubbish tip where they live!

Large trucks collect the rubbish.

Rubbish is taken to landfill sites and buried.

A big problem

Rubbish that is not disposed of properly can cause problems.

People often drop their rubbish on the ground when they are out, instead of looking for a bin. So we get litter on streets and footpaths, in parks and at the beach. Not only is this lazy, but it is also selfish. Would you just drop rubbish on the ground in your garden? Or on the floor in your house? No? Then why would you do it anywhere else?

As well as looking bad, rubbish on the ground can be dangerous. Imagine walking barefoot on the sand at the beach and stepping on a broken piece of glass.

Dropped rubbish is washed away by rain, into rivers and lakes and into the sea. Millions of tonnes of rubbish end up in the world's oceans each year. This rubbish is a danger to marine life. Sea birds, turtles and whales sometimes mistake rubbish for food or become entangled. Rubbish can injure or kill marine life.

Dropped rubbish is a danger to marine life.

Because rubbish can be dangerous, it should always be disposed of correctly.

Don't throw it out

There are many ways to reduce the amount of rubbish you throw away. Here are some things to think about.

Before you buy something, think about whether you actually need it. If you don't really need it, you may end up throwing it out after a while.

Think about the products that you are using. Some items are more wasteful than others. For example, you could take your lunch to school in a reusable container instead of plastic wrap (which is thrown out after use).

If you no longer need something, ask yourself whether it is still useable. If it is, think about selling it or giving it to someone who could use it. Charity shops are always happy to take good donations.

Another important question to ask yourself is – can this item be used for a different purpose? Be creative!

- A plastic shopping bag can be reused during your next shopping visit or as a bin liner.
- Old CDs can be used as drink coasters or in gardens to keep birds away.

- Used corks can be glued together to make a pin board or blended to make mulch.
- Torn clothing can be mended or used to make new items and cleaning cloths.
- Take-away food containers can be washed and reused to store items such as buttons or tea bags.

Nature's waste disposal

Waste is part of the natural cycle of life. Nature has a way of dealing with organic waste and making it useful.

Organic waste is anything that was once alive – leaves and branches that have fallen from trees; animal droppings; animals that have died. All of these things can naturally **decompose**.

During the decomposing process, **nutrients** are released from the waste. The nutrients are then absorbed into the soil, ready to be used by the plants growing there. It's nature's own recycling system.

Bacteria, **fungi** and earthworms all help to break down organic matter. Maggots (fly larvae) also help in the rotting of dead animals.

Earthworms help to break down organic waste.

Useful waste

If you want to make use of your garden waste, the simplest thing to do is to use it as **mulch** or turn it into compost.

Garden waste such as grass clippings can be used as mulch.

Mulch is made from grass clippings or shredded garden waste. It is spread out in a layer over soil to reduce weed growth. It keeps moisture, so if you spread it around plants, you don't need to water them as often. Mulch will eventually break down and return nutrients to the soil.

Composting is an excellent alternative to throwing out organic waste. Food and vegetable scraps can be collected in one area so that worms, bacteria and fungi can do their work and break it down.

The end result is humus – a dark, sweet smelling, nutrient-filled substance that can be added to soil. It will enrich your soil and help your plants grow.

If you can't start your own compost heap, many councils offer garden waste recycling. Special bins are provided into which you can put grass, leaves and cuttings.

Make your own compost

Making your own compost is an easy way to manage household organic waste, and fertilise your garden.

What you need

- garden waste such as lawn clippings and plant cuttings
- kitchen scraps
- a compost bin or a spot in the garden to make a compost pile – you can buy special compost bins from a hardware store or simply turn an old plastic bin upside down and cut out the bottom.

Did you know?

Organic waste is more than just food scraps and garden waste. It also includes:

- paper and cardboard, which is made from trees
- wool, which comes from sheep and other animals such as alpacas
- cotton, which comes from a plant
- hair and nail clippings

All these things can be added to your compost.

What to do

1 Place the bin in an area that has good **drainage** and is shaded during summer.
2 Add food scraps and garden waste into the bin. Cover the scraps with soil. Continue adding your scraps and garden waste.
3 Stir the contents of the bin with a garden stake a few times a week.
4 Wait a few months, before putting the compost onto your garden. You will know it's ready when it has broken down and looks dark brown in colour.

Layer your compost bin with garden waste, scraps and soil.

Helpful hints

Don't place meat, dairy or bread into your compost, as these scraps will attract flies, mice and rats.

Compost needs to be kept moist. If it gets too wet, add some dry scraps, such as leaves or shredded cardboard. If it gets too dry, add a little water.

Recycling

Recycling is the process used to break down materials so that they can be used again to make new products. Many materials can be recycled.

Recycling materials usually takes less energy, water and **resources** than making new materials.

Recycling facts: Glass

Glass containers can be reused and then recycled over and over again.

Recycling glass uses less energy than making new glass. Most glass items in Australia contain at least some recycled glass.

When glass is recycled it is first crushed into a fine powder. It is then melted and mixed with other materials before being made into a new glass product.

All glass jars and bottles are recyclable. Some types of glass, such as light globes, heatproof glass dishes and windowpanes, cannot be recycled in the same way. Do not put them in glass recycling bins.

Recycling facts: Paper and cardboard

Australians use over four million tonnes of paper and cardboard per year. But only about half of that gets recycled.

When paper is recycled, it is broken down into pulp. The pulp is then made into new paper.

It is important to recycle as much paper and cardboard as possible, rather than throw it in the rubbish.

When recycling, it is important not to mix paper with food scraps. This can **contaminate** the recycling process. Paper with food on it, and used tissues, can be placed into your compost instead.

When paper breaks down in landfill, it creates **methane** gas, which is bad for the environment.

Paper and cardboard are made from trees, so by recycling, fewer trees will need to be cut down. In fact, recycling one tonne of paper saves 13 trees. Recycling paper also uses about 50% less energy and 90% less water than making new paper. Paper can be recycled up to eight times.

Recycling facts: Plastic

Plastic is a human-made material and does not break down easily. Even if buried, it will survive for hundreds of years. Therefore it is important to recycle as much plastic as possible.

There are many different types of plastics. Not all plastic can be recycled. Some need to be recycled separately. Not all recycling facilities can handle the different types of plastics, so you need to be careful what you put out for recycling.

Plastics that can be recycled are stamped with a number and symbol. Those labelled 1, 2 or 3 can be put in any plastic recycling bins. You need to check with your local council if they can recycle those labelled 4, 5, 6 and 7.

1 PETE

2 HDPE

3 PVC

It takes less energy to recycle plastic than to create new plastic. The energy saved by recycling one plastic drink bottle could power a computer for 25 minutes.

When recycled, plastics are first sorted into their different types, rinsed and then broken up into little flakes. Then they are melted and re-formed into new plastic items.

Recycling facts: Aluminium

Aluminium is a metal found in a rock called bauxite. Recycling aluminium is important as it takes a lot of energy and resources to manufacture it.

Australia has a good record of aluminium-can recycling. Almost two out of every three cans are recycled.

Aluminium can be recycled over and over again. Each aluminium can that is recycled saves enough electricity to run a TV for three hours.

Recycling facts: Batteries

Recycling batteries is a complex and expensive process. First, they need to be sorted. Then they need to be broken down into their different materials.

Most councils have drop-off locations for battery recycling.

Did you know?

Batteries contain poisonous metals such as cadmium, mercury and lead. They should not be put into the rubbish (landfill) because they can be harmful to the environment.

Cool, clear water

The most used resource in the world is water. We drink it, we wash in it and we use it to grow food.

But water can get dirty and unusable. It can sometimes become a form of waste. How can water be recycled?

The water cycle is nature's way of cleaning water. The sun heats the water in the oceans, rivers and lakes. When heated like this, the water turns into **vapour**, leaving behind everything that was in it (including the salt in sea water).

The water vapour rises and cools. As it cools, it forms droplets that join together to make clouds. When the clouds get heavy, the water falls from them as rain, returning clean water back down to Earth.

The water cycle

Wastewater treatment plant

Rainwater collects in natural **reservoirs** or human-made **dams**. This is what we use as drinking water. Before drinking the water, it goes through a **treatment** plant to remove any dirt. It is filtered (or strained) and chemicals are added to kill the germs.

After water has been used for cleaning, it becomes wastewater. It is carried away from buildings by pipes as sewage. Sewage used to be piped straight into rivers and the sea. This process was bad for the environment.

Today, sewage goes through a treatment plant and is partly cleaned before being released. The partly cleaned water is called effluent and, even though it is not completely clean, it is better for the environment than untreated wastewater.

Recycled water

Wastewater can be recycled – cleaned so that it can be reused. This is particularly important in times of **drought**.

The average Australian household can produce more than 500 litres of wastewater each day. Factories and businesses can produce much more. By recycling some of this water, a lot of drinking water can be saved.

Recycled water is treated to clean it – not as clean as drinking water but clean enough for certain uses.

There are different classes of recycled water, depending on how clean it is – A, B, C and D. Class A is the cleanest.

There are strict rules about how the different classes of water can be used.

Rainwater from your roof can be recycled into the garden.

Uses of recycled water

Class A
• to water food crops • to water gardens and sportsgrounds • for industrial uses where workers could be exposed to the water • to flush toilets • in washing machines • to fight fires
Class B
• for drinking water by farm animals • other industrial uses, e.g. to wash enclosures
Class C
• to grow food for farm animals • in road construction
Class D
• to grow non-food crops, e.g. flowers

Recycling water at home

There are two different types of wastewater produced in homes. Greywater is from kitchens, baths and showers, washing machines and basins. Blackwater is from toilets.

Blackwater cannot be recycled or reused in homes, but greywater can be.

The simplest way to recycle or reuse greywater is to collect it and use it straight away to water your garden. After having a bath, bucket the water out onto your plants. Put a basin into your sink while washing vegetables, then empty it out onto your garden. Anyone can do this!

Some homes install domestic greywater treatment systems. Instead of greywater being put into the sewage system, it is piped into a treatment tank where it can be stored until needed. The tank can be connected to garden hoses and to toilets for flushing.

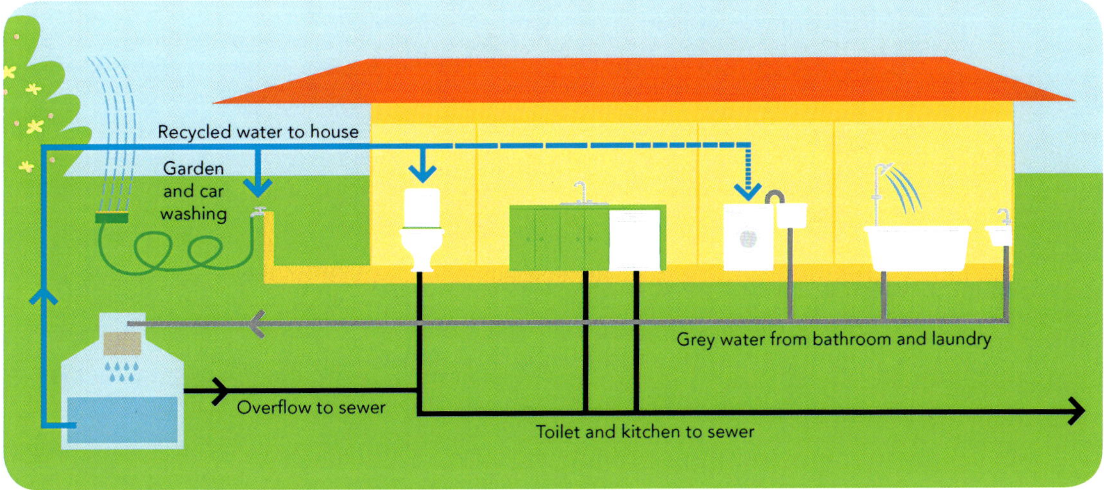

Domestic greywater treatment system

Connections

Think first

Waste is a part of life. But there are many things you can do to reduce waste and landfill. All it takes is a little thought.

Some items can be reused in creative ways.

Think before you buy.
Ask yourself:

- Do I really need this?
- Can I buy less?
- Will it last?
- Is it made from recycled products?
- Can it be recycled?
- How much packaging does it have?

Think before you throw something out.
Ask yourself:

- Can it be reused?
- Can I sell it or give it away?
- Can it be fixed?
- Can it be recycled?
- Can it be composted?

Reduce, reuse, recycle and replace are key actions for a **sustainable** future.

Glossary

bacteria microscopic single-celled life forms

composted broken down vegetable and garden waste

contaminate make dirty or impure

dams walls or barriers built to control the flow of water

decompose break down

drainage removal of water

drought long period of dry weather

fungi spore producing organisms, including moulds and yeasts

methane a colourless, flammable gas

mulch a covering of organic material laid over the soil

non-renewable a resource that is replaced slower than it is used up, such as oil or gas

nutrients substances that provide nourishment and encourage growth

organic from a living thing

pollutes makes dirty or unfit for use

renewable a resource that is replaced as quickly as it is used up or that lasts indefinitely, such as wind or sunshine

reservoirs places where water is collected and stored

resources materials

sustainable long-lived

treatment the removal of bacteria and dirt

vapour particles of moisture

Index